THE SONNETS

Also by Sandra Simonds

Warsaw Bikini
Mother Was a Tragic Girl

THE SONN ETS

by
SANDRA SIMONDS

The Sonnets
© 2014 Sandra Simonds
18 17 16 15 14   2 3 4 5

Design & composition: Shanna Compton, shannacompton.com
Cover design is based on Joe Brainard's "Cover for Ted Berrigan's *The Sonnets*,"
Gouache on paper, 13 x 10, 1964.
Cover texture: Lost & Taken, lostandtaken.com

Published by Bloof Books
www.bloofbooks.com
New Jersey

Bloof Books are printed in the USA by BookMobile. Booksellers, libraries, and
other institutions may order direct from us by contacting sales@bloofbooks.com.
POD copies are distributed via Ingram, Baker & Taylor, and other wholesalers.
Individuals may purchase our books direct from our website, from online
retailers such as Amazon.com, or request them from their favorite bookstores.

Please support your local independent bookseller whenever possible.

ISBN-13: 978-0-9826587-7-2
ISBN-10: 0-9826587-7-X
1. American poetry—21st century. 2. Poets, American—21st century.

∞ This paper meets the requirements of ANSI/NISO Z39.48-1992
(Permanence of Paper).

ONE

TWO

THREE

FOUR

ONE

American Girl

In college I had this job as a file clerk for Dr. Glassman,

    a dentist, whose patients included Brad Pitt and Dodi Fayed

and you probably didn't know that I'm the girl

    who wrote *deceased* with a black Sharpie across the front

of Dodi's chart. Sometimes when I go running my chest hurts

    like a black tunnel in Paris and I've never really thought about who

might write *deceased* across my chart because back then

    I would go surfing in Malibu with my boyfriend and then sleep

on the beach and in the morning, hungover, would take the RTD

    bus back to Beverly Hills to file charts when Tom Petty walks in

and he's so much cooler than Brad Pitt will ever be because yesterday

    in Tallahassee I ran through these trees that had this marijuana-like

smell that reminded me of the way Tom Petty looked when

    I handed him his prescription for antibiotics after he got a filling.

In Reverse Chronological Order, the World Is Formed

Then undone, undid, undo. Into you'll see
  until. No till nor record keeping, no
  tock unbinding. No backward
    grandfather clock unearthing. All shovels
merely confounding, a finding
  out made too late unwinding. The wind
is in this too; it is complicit. Come
  see it with it with it touch it. Too much
wind topples the world like singing Bowie into
a chimney. The world of boats that flip on their sides
  tucking seaside into graveside like a mommy.
Giving and granting, this is my erasure. The ghosts
whip up like furiousness. Above their holes
  they dance and taunt—gigantic at noon.

Because I Have Given Birth

As dilation of cervix   is the soul to blame
   shoot rubber bands   at eggs   like child's play.
   This game's a guinea pig   made of Venetian glass or
   a Third Reich contraction   cast in bronze—
the sperm of the future   the sperm of the past.
Western Civ's Byzantine,   the Red Forest, high alpine passed-
   out cannibal in Donner Party   flag formations.
Oh mini hand   pulled from a flesh hole,   you're the vestigial
   dream of falling   from a tree above
   Swamp Thing.   Children sign off   their forceps-shaped
internet funnels   OB/GYN passwords   stored porn as chat
   or my formyl vagina   still kept mouse-gray in a vat.
Haven't you learned anything   from what won't last?
   Blast that shadow   Sandman casts to glass!

Great Smoky Mountains National Park

My husband calls me a "mountain snob."
"Well, stop leaving empty containers of food
in the cupboards," I respond. It's true.
The Appalachians have nothing
　　on the Sierras. Still, I've dragged him and my son
from Florida to this postpartum cabin
in Tennessee. We sit by a blue lake.
　　We meditate. We sit by a blue river.

Some tweens float by on tires as if rivers and
　　kids are just reels of film. One of them screams
"Help me!" I say I'm too fat to move. The cellulite
　　on my ass won't erode. Call me crazy,
but isn't there a six-week-old infant in my lap?
　　Holy shit, that baby just rolled his eyes at me.

Ode to Marriage

Can we please not talk about Jeffrey Dahmer
    during sex? Wait, that was six family
farms ago. Now I'm single like a piece
    of pineapple in a fruit salad you don't—wait.
Hold on. I'm stuffing walnuts into the carcass
    of a goose because this is a Christian holiday.
I know this because when I turn on the car radio,
    Jesus gives me a weak massage.
(He is friendly, I'll grant him that.)
    Your child runs across the street holding
a dog's skull in his left hand. I take him
    and leave the skull for another driver
to run over. At night, we watch TV together.
    I mean me, you, and the skull.

Young Woman, Prehistoric Mammals Are Not Dinosaurs

I could stay locked in this room listening

    to the Replacements for the next two years.

My right hemisphere's sixteen (blue) and my left one's

    seventy-eight and it's not a question of averaging

the two. Sucks that our common ancestor

    was suicidal as in O sorry-ass fish. O melancholy amoeba.

O despondent mold. But I crawled from sea foam

    into the satin slip of the tongue in expensive

Jungian jeans, the underneath being this year's

    fashion statement. Someday I'll make it

to my little hoof-and-claw forest, wear crinoline antlers,

    felt paws, wrap a patchwork quilt around my form,

wave vacant arms to wild dogs. Another

    phantom. Dumb dumb. I am. Limb.

Bikram Yoga

I was tired because I have a two-year-old son

    so I took some NoDoz and then my heart flipped

out and I needed to relax so I went to a yoga studio.

    And it was like the world was made of awkward

pose. And then life turned Caribbean

    in a headstand. And then I passed

out in underwater aquamarine roses and stars.

 I think the teacher said *plank*,

    which meant I was a pirate in colorful

spandex with a nose ring and booty

    or maybe it meant the world was ending

and soon I'd be flexible—like Zen!

    I hope no one here is concerned—

    the teacher said some poses take a lifetime to learn.

This Is the New Romantic

All the love® I love® turns to shit.

Well, at least I try, goddammit!

I'm talking about the love® of poetry now.

Like how some people hang onto their

poems for so long and then publish them

in the *Nation*. I think it adds love® to value

and value to the love® of nation. Some poets

grow up on expensive farms. They'll tell you about their

chlorophyll childhoods, how easily they led donkeys around

a field. I imagine they become love®'s grassroots activists.

Fuck that shit. Ixnay rich poets,

their collective agrarian past is Pig Latin

to me. This is the new romantic®: I'll post everything

on the internet to devalue® it® for free.

I Love You So So So Sooooooo Much

and after everything I've done ♥ the binary systems mix

    that I've put you through I'm just ♥ their molten cores

happy to relax in Z's room and read him Dr. Seuss ♥ collision course

       and I'm happy in the morning to wait for the garbage truck ♥ X-rays

because Z stands on his toy horse so he can point

    out the window and yell "truck" and I bet I could teach English Comp

forever nothing's ♥ pumped into the galaxy funeral ♥ a rut. I mean

    I know we rot. I rot a lot ♥ the solar system wilts and rots

the seeds we planted they did rot ♥ continents shift because we forgot

    to turn off the hose. We overwatered them. I feel

so dumb so often. Stupid sun! Stupid holes!

    Little beans,

    grow down to hell. There's no beyond ♥

               ♥

               ♥

                   ♥ the earth's core's a blow.

Peruvian Pan Flutes

The trunk of this avocado tree is pink

when dipped in the light of Los Angeles, red

when chillin' in modernity.

Underneath the apartment complex,

there are layers of being: the sea, her empty shells,

plastic Easter grass, concrete, one canvas tennis shoe,

the spit of snails. A man buys a bouquet

of daffodils for his wife hoping she'll have sex

with him. It might work. You can hear her unwrap

the cellophane, open the packet of powdery food, put the flowers

in the vase, while the middle-school-girl next door puts together

a PowerPoint on Anasazi Indians. She just wants a B.

Someone in this dump's always playing the drums.

Pueblos. We spend our entire lives cleaning up.

To Be Verb

The grubs, les shrubs die animals.
 The encrusted goblets the mice eat from,
the sliced-up coconut if this is tropical
  & all is one. Air & beast—
breed religiousness & clip-
clop goes the Clydesdale to town
in 18th century novels where history
is written down. The goat climbs
  into the sun (if this
   is Jerusalem)
 & hills unroll scrolls & scrolls
 of the Pacific's surf. Once I lived
in Los Angeles with her pelican beak
full of fish & is & est & ist.

Shopping Mall Pastoral

World as denim pyramids, permanent makeup,
feathered metal necklaces, the embossed eyebrows
of queen Hatshepsut all over a twenty-dollar miniskirt.
How this aquamarine washable silk dress makes me think
of Lady Lazarus! I'm pregnant in Forever 21
on Friday at three o'clock when all the girls, drunk
on purple rhinestones, line up to try on their cantaloupe-
colored dresses. I think about bloody show,
home birth, touch a faux emerald brooch,
think about how doulas discuss the quality of cervical mucus,
how placenta looks like a cow's soft brain when exposed to a pig's
hysterical hormones, think about how our cows' genetically
altered cells scramble the fields of American eggs
into hot dogs, how everyone eats with four stomachs.

Commemorative Gift

Take raw material drawn from remotest zones: momentum,
Cummingtonite, extract of nightshade, chemicals for pregnancy
tests and then throw them into a locomotive of zeros
that drags the kids by their tunnels into grown-ups.
At home, your child wears wet pajamas with a repeating
Sponge Bob pattern over his chubby thighs.
It's time to change him. The sky above the house
is the closed door of the city's ossified armory.

Thank you for your thirty years of service,
thirty years of pushing the purple and green buttons.
Thank you, bit of emerald placed with tweezers
just left of the three on the wristwatch.
Here's to the jeweler's thumb-finger pincer grasp,
scratched magnifying glass, renewable contract.

Golden Buddha

I'm going to tell you a sonnet and it's going to go by fast, so

you're going to have to listen. It will have a moral. It'll be tight

like a haiku. It will take place when I'm in twelfth grade and I'm going

to be the main character. It is 1994. In this sonnet I will

slip Chinese menus on people's doorknobs

with red and blue rubber bands in Manhattan Beach, California

at the same time I imagine my classmates are slipping on condoms

to prevent themselves from making more of themselves.

This is what I do every day after school to help out my family.

This sonnet sincerely hopes you understand that even though

it's about class and poverty and giving my mom an extra $75 a week

and all of that important stuff that it's also about how this work,

walking from pink house to yellow house to gray house, gave me beautifully

sculpted calf muscles as well as the ability to write this sonnet.

TWO

The Surface

What part of my life is sitting cross-legged in a black cube
full of skylight? The surface, maybe, the philosophy
skimmed like particles of dust
fallen into my water glass next to this out-of-date atlas.
I run my index finger over Bangladesh, the Soviet
Union, the Congo or oak leaves falling into a river
across from the swami who sits cross-legged one
centimeter above the surface of Earth. The worms
move under his form toward the river; the river moves
into a larger body of water; the larger bodies of water pulsate
like pools of blood kept in black cubes. The surface must
be believed like cattle. The surface must be tended to
like farmland underneath mountains that dissolve
and erode, leaving their minerals in our bone.

Baker's Dozen Sci-Fi Sonnet Featuring Charlotte Brontë's Dress Made of an H-O Junk Bond Rating

Mon sem-blah-blah-ounce, this fission sonnet

   is a dumb blonde standing on a melting Mont Blanc

junk bonded to the phrase "O, that I spent my childhood

   in the Alps." Come to think of it, I am an Alp.

Only a hydrogen-peroxide woman would yell

   let me out of the Brontë house. In Haworth, I tried on

Charlotte's dress, my waist's circumference

   a smaller *o* than the nineteenth century where her potential

energy's stored and I thought . . . Indifferent horizon!

   Fizzing fuzz cell hell fusion cuisine string theory!

Bomb of was, you never were! Us girls put petroleum byproducts

   on our lips to kiss Swiss chocolate. That yelp alp

is anorexic. Atomic mass diet. Synthesis. Mon, whatever.

Corduroy Shingles

Of course the surface is crumbling into marriage swans
all along the lakes and waterways of their corn-fed suburb.
Still, there is hope for landscape architecture, bewilderment,
a chance to throw slices of cheap bread into the duck ponds or
take them to the children's museum before it will close for good
or to the library before it will close for good.
Their parents, cellular, don't know how to respond
when they ask about the difference
between prehistoric mammals and dinosaurs.
A well-respected PTA dad keeps saying, "You're the man,"
every time his son hits the ball into the blinking atmosphere.
Now they are cursors. Some even paint their toenails
"apocalypse" pink. Or precursors. When day is done, they teach
their children to count sheep into the serial night.

Black Friday

There *really is* a place in my register for you.
    It's too bad your heart has become
like a machine, counting shapes and sizes
    the way pornography rolls inside
   the eyeballs of the habitual viewer
or maybe the way this sales assistant folds never-
worn shirts. One is lavender and the dye
    pools into the open areas of the terrible
shopping mall. To shout, "This is hell!"
      over children and samples of Chinese food.
That the shopping mall sits in the small
    hand of the valley and that the valley
is filled with the cool, nameless skin
    of lovers walking away—oh world reptilian.

House of Ions

See my life's collection of fossils on the mantle
   above the fireplace? In this photo, I'm standing inside
    the phosphorus origin of a second-rate pyramid
     and in that one—my useless attempt
at making pineapple upside-down cake.
 From stone to state, death to the nursing home,
from what's been to glass bottles of vitamins, through adulthood's
   prescriptions for antidepressants left unfilled,
then nursing a bottle of beer in the full health
   of Florida beside the turtle-shaped plastic pool,
back through the milky nipple of newborn motherhood,
   the flushed cheeks of college. How the electrolytes
shake the eyes into a house of ions, sarcophagus,
   box of solar dirt. Sight usurped by continuous labor.

Safe House Safe

Hello there. Welcome to my safe house.

Here you will find numerous porcelain Afghanistans.

In the safe house safe there are coins cut in the shape

of Malawi. In the study where I wish you to relax, please

find a number of wood carvings of John Lennon & Sons.

The lampshades are German. The Persian rugs are tongue.

Kind sir, halt! Do not issue another fatwa in Farsi!

Not until you consider my landscape painting of Trebižat, that great

Bosnian river or Smith's high-realist triptych of the Tunguska event.

Hello there. It would please me to please you with kindness

upon entering my safe house door. If anything should

irradiate the staff, there are replacement servants

ready in waiting to greet you beside the blown-up photos

of gargoyles on the veranda in the cosmic burst garden.

Collapsible Sledgehammer

Documentary films are so boring.

It's like people going on about the gold standard (yawn).

And for whatever reason they remind me of Tonya Harding's

ex-husband hiring that man to break

Nancy Kerrigan's bronze leg. . . . BTW, has anyone

here ever taken ice-skating lessons? . . .

To be fair, I don't give a crap about the cinema;

I don't even consider it art. In this interview

http://www.youtube.com/watch?v=YrKK9v-RoIk

Werner Herzog thinks women don't understand

the "exhilaration" of being shot. But when you imagine

Why-why-why-Kerrigan simultaneously

watching *Grizzly Man* and auctioning her historic

knee on eBay you can only say, "Herzog, I think not!"

T-Shirt Bought at Borders with Shakespeare's Face on It

Master Sand in Mistress Will and Master Will
    in Mistress Sand. People will say we're not a man
but Sand's wed to her debt is willed to her sand.

Take it from Will, Sand's heir is sand, dispersants
    in air, seahorse bikini, layers of crustacean sediment.

Will and I will you a bag of sand dollars since
    we're on the Gulf, oysters in the *r* months,
ambulance sirens spiraling to loan debt that goes
    into repayment long before you're born.

All the world's the offspring of Will's spill, a tampon
    dunked in Russian vodka, a drunk slave song chemical pump,
Botox injected into the radiant cheeks of the city dump.

Take it from Sand's taught English Comp all
day long to become Master of Will's mutant lung.

The Seafarer

Whose core? Quorum's core. Whose core? Corium's core.

    I mean the emperor's totally hardcore

shoreboard. Score! Who's more? He's more. Who's more?

He's more. That's what this emporium sonnet's for.

    I don't remember which of you has the best

pelvic floor. I mean is this the floor of the reactor or

        is this a Sanskrit message written in agribiz's soil?

No more. I'm cured. Or five-hour energy drink

    need to run to the store.

Bodies as arboreal energies galore whore.

      Bodies as there's room on my living room floor whore.

   In Fukushima at night I mean in Des Moines

     the erudite I mean things that bob like jellyfish.

     Like astronauts. Like dogs.

No Sonnet

No Civil War sonnet. No sex reassignment surgery sonnet.

No Black sonnet. No climate change sonnet.

No.

No crossed-out Unitarian Universalist sonnet.

No African-American sonnet. No girly sonnet.

No boyish lip gloss sonnet.

No crime spree sonnet. No egret sonnet.

No machete sonnet. No.

No adorable sonnet. No iron-on patch sonnet.

No Crimean War memorabilia sonnet.

No Greek laurels sonnet.

No.

No consignment store sonnet.

No global diamond store sonnet.

Lace Clouds over House over House over House over House

A dirty diaper on the bathroom floor
   and my toddler taking a bath, his father washing
his little back with a yellow sponge plucked from the sea.
    There are submerged mountains taller
        than Mount Everest in the sea. Google it.
   Life and her frail salinity seem slow, saintly even,
at this time in the evening or ponderous like
    the whale shark who circled the tank
at the Georgia Aquarium when we went to visit.
    The children and their parents, holding hands,
moving through the engineered fish, point at
   deep time's thick glass walls separating
single-celled organisms from
   complexity, awe.

Black Leotard

There was one man, then two men, then three.

    The worst part of me did a somersault on the balance beam.
The bumblebee audience cooked to 103 degrees.
One man bumped the next one off the beam, then the next

    one did the same thing. I spent the day making sure I didn't call
each one by the wrong name. When the married man talked about

    his wife, I cringed. When my husband threatened to take

    his own life, I cringed. When the man who was the innocent
bystander of all this didn't say anything, the Russian judge

    gave him points he didn't deserve out of pure fidelity. Then they called
my name and I knelt before all three, as the winner put the bronze

    medal over my head. This book is a fable. It is an Old English riddle.
Want some? It is also a koan: she who is wise puts

    down breadcrumbs, never plays dumb, gets home before sunrise.

Immense Fields of Work

Waking up to the gray farm redoubles your doubts.

     All fall down. "Tucker?"

A row of cantaloupes in the garden freaking you out

       like rippled faces where narcissus French kisses

the infested pond. They dreamed and they dreamed

     and they dreamed of out west, antelope, log cabins,

but rats scratched their way through the arteries

       of their lives. "I can sing really well," I told Tucker.

     "Fucker!" he said when he stubbed his toe on

my guitar. It was a warm day and the next

       day was warmer. Each cold storm had, at its

center, a hollow fruit. Then I opened the window, saw

     a stranger smashing the cantaloupes with that guitar.

     Seeds everywhere seeds. Six strings.

Dismantle the Cradle

We couldn't find the peach tea, rattle, atlas,

plastic *Tyrannosaurus rex*, so we moved on.

   This is what geologists call *the surface*,

but what about the surfeit underneath

   the white caps of cells, daffodils, oceans, skulls?

We lost a child too young to yawn at us,

   learned the mind must be formed to be bored.

And what if there is lava?

   And what if there's a bundle

of neurons deep within Earth's iron core?

   Never mind. Leave all the beta particles behind.

We lost houses too. And churches, synagogues,

   favorite taco stands, and photos that must

somehow prove I loved you and you and *you*.

THREE

Over Nothing

So what if a man hits a woman in the throat?
    She's not as beautiful as she once
was anyway. Her "power of refusal"
        over prawns. Over steak? Over grilled
halibut? Over nothing. The dinner candles twist
more than Mulholland Drive, the restaurant's
      sommelier pours Los Angeles into crystal,
        the couple leaves the Valley in a car, crosses a decade
but the problem is the same with different people
wearing the same clothes with different people's
      eyelashes fluttering the Great Plains
    in between their hands. Like space
  when the whole city breaks into the foaming
red face of seawater on the edge of a sandy cliff.

Come Back!

What did I do
        to push you away?
  I know that I talk a lot and I'm always on Twitter
and Facebook. This is not the way a good woman
      should be reserved but I'm all impulse
    and want to show you my house and my garden see
I planted those beans myself and the tomatoes I ordered the seeds
      off the internet and planted them and now I'm emailing you
all the time and I just want to talk on the phone or something.
    Sometimes I think about home-schooled Walter at the playground
   and he's just starved for attention but he's four years old,
     not a woman with black hair, blue eyes and a failing marriage.
    Come back! I'll let you play with my trains, make you some oolong tea,
      do your laundry, tell your future in tarot cards.

Exploding Florida

Like your husband saying "Good luck with your life,"
    a rare Florida orchid gets drunk on doomsday
at noon on what looks like a Middle English green,
      between a toddler in Spider-Man pajamas who jumps
from the trampoline set up on the front lawn
      onto a cactus plant and his mother, mom
        mama, more of her more of her gaga,
boo-boo, kiss-kiss, more of her scandalous life stripped
      to a naked plot twist, more fleshy Florida
    where even the anesthetic used to numb, pull
out the cactus needle is sucking and sexing.
    All the pink sands of the universe
funnel through this mess of narcotic clouds
  that burst like bodies, that burst their own children.

Animal Kingdom

Make me a mutant cannon of DNA you can't rein in,
    a carrier pigeon cannon formed
        of decomposed Morse code, hoarfrost on the chromo-
            some boats, the eyehole
                bones of an abandoned woman's hello or the unborn.
                Next, make me a lost mutt by
                    calling animal control. Put fur in one corner
                and then follow her wag to the shelter. In your sonic
                boom sonnet, spaniel and dachshund will howl
                    allele spirals until they breed dumb or smart, medium
                        or three-legged pigeon with woof. Make me
    an earful of unusual bird dogs, the left-for-dead
    in fool's gold, the side-of-the-road way he
    looks at you when he wants to go home. *Hello?*

Existence Mustn't Flinch

The *Aloe vera* plant, spiky lament, never talks

directly about despair,

is the biggest lie of human nature

and nature is not the plant

we want to hear soothes a sunburn

when we talk about the beach

it has to mean something like the last

step off the plank of space

onto the plank

of dissonance, like the hermit crab—that cutie pie—

who pops back into her shell

when she's scared of the feathered tide or

the human finger—so extraordinarily large

against the bald baby skull of noon.

Playing House

Just you and the knots
    up the rope throat to
the tree house into your
    room of worn-out things.
  The garbage bag leaks fermenting juice.
      Can I bring you a cup of coffee,
  the newspaper, a noose? The moon is out, brighter
  than any idea either one of us
will have. I would take a sledgehammer to it
  pound out your name if you had one.
   O you like a trick, the electronic stars, like a copycat plague
  who has already written this poem
in the same world one over.
    (Dedicated to this poem.)

Buffalo '66

The internet's teeth chatter

sounds like typing 80 wpm on the ice plane

of the stupidest memory of Vincent Gallo

handing Dr. Glassman the "artsy" photographs

OF A SCONE

yes, a cranberry scone in black and white

that he took at the next-door coffee shop.

The cranberries looked like black flies eating their own birthplace

and how would I know that? Because when I thought everyone

had left, I opened the door of Dr. Glassman's private office

and touched and inspected each photo, each rounded scone

like I was touching Vincent's celebrated cheeks

and then Kathy, the hygienist, crept in

and said, "All he wanted was sex."

I'm Miss World, Somebody Kill Me

Brad Pitt does not want to be Brad Pitt any more than anyone else
wants to wait for the dentist—birthplace of primal fear.
So get a Coke or something. Why so attached
to your megalomania? I had cut my hair
like Gwyneth Paltrow around the time she was in *Great Expectations*—
when Pitt comes in and says,
"Someone is following me."

1. Pip works in the forge unhappily.
2. A lawyer named Jaggers appears with strange news.
3. Pip must come to London *immediately* to get an education.
   O large fortune dwindling down like your wife's wedding dress
   in the tornado drain below the earth's surface
   when the bride dances at noon—that empress
   of all things. Someone is *always* following you.

Camp Vagina Lake

Every day is like the last day of us. The crises
more tenacious than the pathetic eighth-grader
    assigned *Beowulf.* She is a good student
but lame. When a boy kisses her
at water ski camp after she almost kills a fellow camper
    with the pointed tip of her water ski, she'll
blush and when he doesn't look at her
      the next day, her heart will explode.
      Splash goes the water ski accident
right into the other girl's Hello Kitty chest.
    A friend will teach her how to put a tampon in, everyone will eat
    marshmallows and sing through their braces
      and their awkward song will be swallowed
by the Sierras, full of Grendels closing in.

Fruit in Warehouse

In high school I lost Dylan Klebold
a girlfriend over Dylan Klebold
a disagreement over Dylan Klebold
the meaning of the first Dylan Klebold
paragraph of Dylan Klebold
of page one of *Klebold's Rainbow*
which is a perfectly good Dylan Klebold
reason to Dylan Klebold
oranges, tomatoes and pears are best
bought on organic Dylan Klebold
farms think wholesale Dylan Klebold
Dylan Klebold, first love
Dylan Klebold, affair
Dylan Klebold, lovechild

Lines Written in the Back of a Police Car in Chicago, Illinois

Like Hearst's castle, the earth's gilded falsehoods:
        the fall of man, the apple, the rats scattering
across history books. History—our brainchild,
our criminal. Where is the Fountain of Youth?
        Where are the breadcrumbs, the clues?
The policeman says, "I'd like to live in Montana
        and around my life I'll dig a moat and fill
        that moat with crocodiles and fill
        the crocodiles' mouths with human flesh."

What kind of century is this? XY? XX?
        Pages of excess enter the heart and exit
    medieval cobblestone. A skeleton key,
        the opposite of bone, of mass. All day
        in pepper spray he says, "I give. I get. I own."

Two Bicycles: One Plain, One Fanciful

I made you things. Things that
move I made up made up things of milkmaids
    with my mothering I strung an oud
  out of the vow-like fingertips I plucked
the music to prove cows roam pasture: see they
      do for you I drew the spokes, the seats, the handlebars
    that fit into the grip of Pasteur's hypotheses stored in a vault
        with that which causes rabies, anthrax tucked it in with
Jenner's accomplishments. Hear this: all pasture is gigantic
with humping! Everything is clear vaccine pushed into
toddler fat! *Stay alive*, the needles say. And when the clock
strikes five, the depressed nurse with the beehive rides
    home on a bicycle she doesn't own thinking,
    Oh Sandman, you mess, can't you give it a rest?

Jórvík

You were working at the hospital, having recently
graduated from college. And there was Marisa
    on the fourth floor, the most beautiful girl from high school
with a nurse standing on either side of her.

The neuropsychiatric institute made her flat face
look historic, Norse. Saga-white fumes of antipsychotics
    in the air like ancient tools. You looked away, Sandra, but
oh she recognized you from the night you dropped acid
    and went to see the *Dark Side of the Moon*
        laser show at the planetarium in Hollywood.

      Flesh survives forever in peat.
    I've seen the wheat-colored hair of the bog people
at museum exhibits. I have pressed my cheek to the glass
case of the missing. Marisa, could they be you?

Lincoln Logs

"We are making some fine universe,"

    my five-year-old says, "with sheer will."

Wind shear on an airplane's wing can be horrible.

    You open your laptop and the crash

is Russian or African, so it doesn't matter.

    If there's a morgue behind the pizza parlor

      you frequent, the five-year-old will notice.

He will clap his diminutive hands, say, "We are making some fine

      universe out of what we have." The guy throws

    the dough into the air and it spins like the number of reasons

      we hold one another close. The dead man still

has toes. You leave the parlor like you're walking out

of the Taj Mahal seeing a monkey lick his paw

      and yes, you are now a glacier.

FOUR

American Songs

This was going to be a gorgeous crown
    of sonnets about atoms and bombs.
To tell you the truth, though, I don't know jack
    about crowns or Adam and Eve. But isn't that what's
awesome about being an American poet?
    You can just take your ignorance
and run with it or rename it *bravado*.
    You can just say, "History, you're a ho," and then
Lady Mary Wroth will crawl back
    into her English hole. Everything
I say here I own. I'm my own
    master of this here zone. I write
what I sing like karaoke. I sing what I write
like Kryptonite.

Adios, Adonis

I wanted love—not deceit. Eat shit,
    deceit! I've got to update my CV.

My grandmother's got Parkinson's disease.
    In a poem about deceit, shouldn't the poet

use the word *eaves*? Okay, now I'm eavesdropping
    on my own life, my little twisted ear pressed

to the hardwood floor of it, looking into the crack
of light spilling out from under its bedroom door.

Don't cry, señorita, I tell myself. Behind
that door sits Helen of Troy, gorgeous ploy, employ,

yo-yo, guy toy, chew toy rolling her au-revoir eyes
    and then throwing the scroll of her stupid life overboard

because she knows the only way to score Mexico is
    to contort deceit to stone.

Into the House of Love

The landlady informs me she owes me hundreds of dollars.

   Apparently, I've been overpaying her for months.

What she doesn't know is I'm building a house for her as a present.

     Inside the house, there will be a colorful tomb.

   I will push her into this colorful tomb.

She doesn't know it yet. I have so many tricks up my sleeve.

    It's because I'm passive-aggressive. It's because I'm mean and violent.

Have you built a house with a colorful tomb at its center yet?

   The sea has a center. And everyone loves the sea

    because the sea loves no one. She pulls in everything: the nursery,

      the moon, the glass of milk the moonlight

shines through on the kitchen counter.

    If I had to compare the sea to something

I'd compare her to the sea.

Master of Fine Arts

When I was a student getting my MFA,
  the psychologist I was seeing gave me a piece
of paper that was a gigantic list
  of writers who committed suicide.

I'm not sure if he was trying to say that I'm in
good company or that I'm all alone.
  When I left the appointment, I climbed the hill
  adjacent to the university, the one with the M

carved into it. I've never understood this need
for humans to carve letters into hillsides—like saying
"Mother, I am here and alive," and then
  I thought about how my first year of college

  I came home to find my mother's body
after she had swallowed a bottle of pills.

Ducks Floating Serenely across Pond Make Scenery Serene

Fuck all I say I say fuck all.
Fuck fruit fuck man fuck beast fuck herb.
Fuck you fuck him fuck the mandarin
orange, the clementine, my darling,
fuck the wine that's fucked me up
and fuck the fuck
and fuck the what-the-fuck
and fuck the computer, the stingray
and the sun that dips into the ocean.
Fuck all I say say all I fuck.
Fuck the octopus, the kangaroo,
the summer grass, idiotic and swirling
like a mind of neurons that look as lost
and despondent as sperm in tissue.

A Sonnet for *Warsaw Bikini*

I call sand holy though I know no place

    but Earth and sometimes I lie down in the beached

 grasses of the brain where a lizard hangs and the sun it does

hit the back and turn it brown and then when I get home

and take a shower all that's left are the white

    lines of my bikini straps like pure rib bone.

Would you be so kind as to bury me in my tan lines,

     those negative ribbons that stretch to Saturn, to the white dwarfs,

to Neptune, nocturne and place a gold coin on my lizard tongue

     so that I do not talk a lot? *Goddamn*, I talk a lot!

Tick-tock. I rot. *Do too. Do not.* The centrifugal force of tongue

    mocks her own vortices, makes all our

    voices half whore half shepherdess, pushes it

     through this garbled and glittering vacuum.

Garden of Earthly Delights

The daycare worker tells me to be careful,

  that there is a rabid gray fox

    on the loose. After I drop off my son,

      I go for a run. There are many women walking.

   They hold black umbrellas over their heads to protect

their bodies from our nearest star as if there were a way to shield

       oneself from the messy galaxy of the human heart.

I imagine each body has a story it must protect,

     each story has a complicated protagonist who would

     narrate the golden life of the flesh if it didn't hurt

  so much—the cliffhangers as well as the boring

    passages where people are just sitting in a mahogany

drawing room, Victorian, drinking Earl Grey

  from porcelain cups with painted roses and foxes on them.

Personal Credit Score

I'm afraid, sir, we've been unable to locate your biological mother.

    Deep within the numeric garden: decay, irreverence, frost

    and your father who takes a cartoon pocketknife and slices

right through the $ sign on six bags of gold. No Eve yet.

    Out spills an auditorium of zoo sounds—

      honks, trills, whistles as well as ordinary

men and women, each one assigned a number

    floating above his or her head. Number

    and ghost, ghost and man. At the movies,

 we gather to watch the last piece of the 3-D ship slide into arctic

waters in the same way your birth century has silently

  passed through the cold turnstiles of history or the way the gilded

side of a three-tier wedding cake slumps beneath the Mojave sun:

      the world an uneaten apple.

The Sum

If you don't respect love, it won't respect you.

In the other room, I'm pretty sure Jason's on the phone

with his drug dealer. Actually, even if you *do* respect love,

it doesn't give a fuck. Jason just asked me if I want to go

play tennis. I don't know if I have the energy

to smash particles together. Jason's a lie.

I'm an accelerator. He didn't smite three beasts

with the flex of his thumb. We play tennis with protons:

I'm dumb I'm love I don't know maybe

I'm wearing the cutest white miniskirt

with a green turtle embroidered on it. What truth aside

from blowout, bolson, bond, brackets, rackets,

until the only thing that matters is

the sun, his drugs, the telephone.

Japan

Will's gone. Sandman's strong. Will's near the fear I fear
    is faster than the man who swims to his wife
    in a sea of irradiated silverware, pufferfish,
Honda Accords. Do the cheeks of Hondas bulge
    at night; does roe fall like snow into the glow-in-the-dark waters?
      Koan: How many moons roll silently on the sea floor?
Koan: Do you think the surface of your life will tumble towards me
    like hurricane season? Sand's language is Finnish;
Will's is Dutch. Finished! Enough! Now Sand's got the Indo-European
touch and Will's a crybaby with the croup. Smack him. Shake him—
    don't let him regroup when he splits off into Will and Sand's gone.

    Will's strong. Take every neutron you've earned
    and put it in your will, your sonogram, your urn, your flipped-
out hourglass of undulating sand from the sea's rough surfaces.

Mixtape

Shiva diva with a shiv. Skeezer Shiva
    knows what she do and doesn't giva.
Matryoshka doll Shiva taking off her painted shells
    until she's solid, smells like spray paint
on the side of a NOLA-bound freight straight into
    Katrina mold. God-willing gangsta uncurling her
    Insha'Allah fingers. She ain't no holla back girl
with broken acrylic tips going to 7-Eleven to buy Bubble Yum
    to take to hon, doesn't get shitfaced on Assange's tweets
or crunk on the dumb lotus flower yoga pose. Shiva diva
    rascal's meaner shimmying across Himalayan stage
like she's Sir Edmond Hillary, the flapper. Itty bitty piggy
Shiva shivers—don't let her get ya, carjack Shiva.
    Master killa so she killa master.

The Soul as Lo-Fi Diva

It is a good thing, to be sure, that there is a soul and that,
    though fragile, she looks around and isn't easily frightened.
       Maybe this is because she is housed so deep
within the flesh or maybe it is because
    she is so flamboyant with her leopard skin
tights and Doc Martens and wolf-skull necklace.
    And it is funny how she will only
talk to you when in despair. She is so snobbish!
She wears your grandmother's fur coat and bracelets made
of inchworms. She wears watermelon lip gloss and licks her lips
      to a metronome set to civil disobedience. She's not going
to bother you when you're at the bar talking to that cute
guy you want to screw. She won't get all up
    into your business. She knows her place.

Into the House of Florida

You are my ounce, my octagon, my omen, ornate
    as palm leaf shadow curing the chlorinated waters
of the nuclear family's backyard swimming pool.
They own the world, do they not? You are my zero-sum game,
    my tribe, sailboat catching its cloth lip on the torn horizon.
You are my minus sign, my timeline, mathematic as water stored
    in a cube of antimatter. You open the cube
and poof—the genie, wearing a powdered wig, is out!
    You weigh organism. You weigh organ. You oscillate.
You climb into an oasis and come out as-is. As is always.
    You dream of Nazi werewolves. I don't listen. You drive to Orlando.
    To Tampa. It is night. The bats' sonar systems
        pulsate below our ozone, our little homeostatic zones
        reverberate like blood or home.

Red Wand

Sometimes I try to make poetry, but mostly

    I try to earn a living. There's something still living

in every urn, I am sure of it. The ash moves

      around inside the vase like the magnetic filings that make

the moustache of Wooly Willy. Maybe a new face counts

    as reincarnation. The wand says, "I'll be your ostrich,

if you'll be my swan." In this life, what did I do wrong?

I think my heart is a magnet too. It attracts anything

    that attracts joy like the summer grasses the swans track through.

    OMG, how in love I am with joy and with yours—how I know

that adding to it would only take it further off course,

    off its precarious center, so for once, I won't touch it.

I will stand wand-length away—let it

    glide stupidly on its weightless line, without me.

Acknowledgments

The author and publisher thank the editors of the following publications, who first published these poems:

Academy of American Poets, Poets.org/Poem-a-Day: "Red Wand"

The Awl: "Animal Kingdom" and "Over Nothing"

Barrelhouse: "Because I Have Given Birth" and "Immense Fields of Work"

Barn Owl Review: "Two Bicycles: One Plain, Once Fanciful," "Adios, Adonis," "The Sum," "Exploding Florida," "Existence Mustn't Flinch," "I'm Miss World, Somebody Kill Me," and "A Poem for *Warsaw Bikini*"

Better Magazine: "Black Leotard"

Boston Review: "Golden Buddha"

The Brooklyn Rail: "Corduroy Shingles," "The Surface," and "Commemorative Gift"

Court Green: "Shopping Mall Pastoral," "Prehistoric Mammals Are Not Dinosaurs," "The Surface," "Lace Clouds Over House Over House Over House," "Bikram Yoga," "Give Me Space," "American Girl," "Great Smoky Mountains National Park," "Ode to Marriage," "House of Ions," "This Is the New Romantic," "Collapsible Sledgehammer," "American Sonnets," and "In Reverse Chronological Order, the World Is Formed"

Everyday Genius: "No Sonnet" and "Into the House of Florida"

Housefire: "Lincoln Logs," "Japan," "Camp Vagina Lake," and "Garden of Earthly Delights"

Ilk Journal: "Lines Written in the Back of a Police Car in Chicago, Illinois," "Dismantle the Cradle," and "Playing House"

Juked: "Master of Fine Arts," "Buffalo '66"

Lemon Hound: "Young Woman, Prehistoric Mammals Are Not Dinosaurs," "Golden Buddha," "Black Leotard" and "Lines Written in the Back of a Police Car in Chicago, Illinois"

Open Letters Monthly: "Peruvian Pan Flutes"

Please Excuse This Poem: 100 Poets for the Next Generation: "Golden Buddha"

Pool : "I Love You So So So Soooooo Much," "To Be Verb," "Into the House of Love," "Jórvík"

Sixth Finch: "Personal Credit Score"

Verse Daily: "Great Smoky Mountains National Park"

About the Author

Sandra Simonds is the author of two previous collections of poetry, *Warsaw Bikini* (Bloof Books, 2008) and *Mother Was a Tragic Girl* (Cleveland State University Poetry Center, 2012). Her poems have appeared in *The Best American Poetry 2014*, the *American Poetry Review*, *Fence*, *Poetry*, and other journals.

Praise for *THE SONNETS*

Sandra Simonds's sonnets are so good I couldn't stop reading them. Though they skirt the surface (young mother, wife, shopping mall, classroom), they are driven by a seeming impulsiveness and a bravura, as well as a kind of scientific lyricism, that put you in touch with the cosmic abyss. But it's pointless to try to describe these sonnets. You need to experience for yourself their acuity and their mystery. —**David Trinidad**

What is a sonnet? It is a thing that only loves to be exactly itself, like Richard Simmons, isn't it? Not so fast. In Sandra Simonds's new book, the sonnet has escaped, runs wild, scavenges for itself. She stands in the landscape where it lives, noticing, an older form even than the sonnet is, and present behind her are megaflora and megafauna, and in front of her are all the small arrayed things of the new world that have been laid out for her to observe: "We are making some fine universe, / my five year old says, with sheer will. We are making some fine / universe out of what we have. —**Patricia Lockwood**

Like her earlier work, Sandra Simonds's *The Sonnets* is fierce. I want my boyfriend to read them. I want my mom to read them. I want the police to read them, and weep. I wish I could do the things she does in this book—technically, politically, intellectually—but then I'd have to stop writing poems, they are that alive. They make me want to jump up. —**Chris Nealon**

Sandra Simonds's new poems dizzy, as usual. This time, the vertiginousness is nested inside the lush ersatzitude of the sonnet. Her sonnets are traditional, if tradition says that sonnets are half-legible mimeos, a gift of beau désordre, evidence of how interestingly replication degrades. Floating tweens, Tom Petty, junk bonds, turtle shaped-pools, failing marriages, and Facebook make this book a classic upender of the classic. —**Anne Boyer**

CPSIA information can be obtained
at www.ICGtesting.com
Printed in the USA
LVHW041250041118
595902LV00003B/575